DILBERT'S GUIDE TO THE REST OF YOUR LIFE

DILBERT'S GUIDE
TO THE REST OF YOUR LIFE

Dispatches from Cubicleland

RUNNING PRESS
PHILADELPHIA • LONDON

9 8 7 6 5 4 3 2 1
Digit on the right indicates the number of this printing

Library of Congress Control Number 2006921031

ISBN-13: 978-0-7624-2781-9
ISBN-10: 0-7624-2781-7

Cover and interior design by Frances J. Soo Ping Chow
Edited by Greg Jones
Typography: Brush Script, Futura, and Metallophile

This book may be ordered by mail from the publisher.
Please include $2.50 for postage and handling.
But try your bookstore first!

Running Press Book Publishers
2300 Chestnut Street
Philadelphia, PA 19103

Visit us on the web!
www.runningpress.com

Visit Dilbert on the web!
www.dilbert.com

TABLE
OF
CONTENTS

Introduction

YOU RECEIVED THIS BOOK as a gift because someone noticed that you're about to enter the business world
with a solid education and plenty of idealism. That is the
equivalent of using a hanky to skydive.

This book will teach you how to roll into a ball and cover yourself with a temporary coating of distrust and cynicism. In time you will acquire something called "experience" to dull your senses. Until then, this book is your best protection against the series of low-grade misfortunes you will later call a career.

I extend to you my condolences, but more importantly, I give you the priceless advice on the pages that follow. These nuggets of wisdom are plucked from the input of thousands of cubicle-dwellers who came before you. Most of those people are still in cubicles, slowly decaying in their clothes. So they know what they're talking about.

Many young people think that Dilbert is just a comic strip. You are about to discover that it's actually your biography, somehow creepily written in advance. I wish you the best of luck navigating the business world, and I hope that *Dilbert's Guide to the Rest of Your Life* gets you off to a safe start.

—Scott Adams

CAREER DAY

WHEN YOU GROW UP
YOU'LL BE PUT IN A
CONTAINER CALLED
A CUBICLE.

Chapter 1

GETTING HIRED
AND GETTING STARTED

THE BLEAK OPPRESSIVE-
NESS WILL WARP YOUR
SPINE AND DESTROY
YOUR CAPACITY TO
FEEL JOY.

LUCKILY, YOU'LL HAVE
A BOSS LIKE ME TO
MOTIVATE YOU WITH
SOMETHING CALLED
FEAR.

MAY I SEE
A BROCHURE?

The job interview process is designed to be as humiliating and degrading as possible. It weeds out the whiners. Save your whining for later when you've created the illusion of being indispensable.

DON'T WORRY about your job qualifications. Your potential boss would hire a monkey with a drinking problem if the monkey had a good haircut. All you have to do is pretend you aren't worthless for the duration of the interview.

f your college degree has the word "arts" in it

anywhere, you'll have no problem getting a job,

at least as long as cars and dishes get dirty.

The best jobs are the ones that involve talking nonsense to people who can't tell the difference. Avoid jobs that involve moving objects or accomplishing measurable objectives.

CAREERS ARE what Vikings and blacksmiths had. Your "career" will be a series of random jobs that are each somewhat less horrible than the one before. Eventually, when you have changed jobs enough times, you will be old.

Try to work
with people who are
even more useless
than you.
It makes you look
spectacular.

No one hates you more than the people who have to train you. They don't get paid extra to do it and they would consider it embarrassing if you learned their entire job in an hour.

I LIKE TO START EACH DAY BY SENDING THREATENING E-MAIL TO THE BOARD OF DIRECTORS.

Learn to speak gibberish. It's easier than

acquiring knowledge and it will put you on

the management fast track.

CARING ABOUT the quality of your work causes stress. Stress can kill you. Maintain good health by remembering that the stockholders are complete strangers who have never done anything for you.

CAN YOU TEACH ME TO BE APATHETIC LIKE YOU?
ONLY IF YOU HAVE A STRONG DESIRE NOT TO LEARN.

Chapter 2

CO-WORKERS

THERE'S NO POLITE WAY to tell a coworker to leave

your cubicle. Your best bet is to say you have a meeting

and then hide in a restroom stall until the coast is clear.

IT'S EASY TO TELL which of your coworkers are

tragic bores; they're the ones who are talking.

I f money doesn't buy happiness, you might wonder

why the people who are paid the least are always

the most disgruntled.

HUMOR IN THE WORKPLACE is a good way to improve

morale, not counting the people you are laughing at.

You might find your soul mate at work. That will be your first clue that there's something seriously wrong with your soul.

Every group has at least one sadistic loser who is trying to grab your ankles as he circles the drain. If you can't identify someone like that in your group, you probably already have your hands on someone's ankles.

IT'S A GOOD IDEA to accuse coworkers of heinous acts before they do the same to you. That way their credibility will be in question when you have to explain why you've been selling pallets of printer paper on eBay.

The less you know
about what
your coworkers are
thinking, the happier
you will be.

Chapter 3

MANAGEMENT

Maturity is understanding that you are not the center of the universe and that you don't know everything. If that doesn't work for you, try management.

If you steal
a little
bit of money,
you are a criminal.
If you steal
a lot, you're a
leader.

f you label people "headcount," it makes it easier to abuse them later without wondering if you have turned into some sort of monster.

YOU CAN DETERMINE your value to the company by timing how long your boss stays on the phone when you are sitting in his office. Anything over an hour is a bad sign.

IF YOU WORK HARD, your boss will recognize how

much harder he worked when he was your age.

DID I EVER TELL YOU ABOUT MY FIRST JOB AS AN ENVELOPE LICKER?
CLICK

Nothing that you tell your manager will be as important to him as the things he's hallucinating while you are talking.

WHEN YOU FEEL THE URGE to pound your boss on the

head—and you will—try to do it metaphorically.

A leader's goal
is to convince
employees that
insincere gratitude
is every bit
as valuable as cash.

t's a good idea to pretend you are indeed

motivated by slogans and tee shirts, because

the alternative will be worse.

THEN HOW COULD YOU POSSIBLY MOTIVATE US TO SAY WE'RE HAPPY TO WORK...UH-OH.

Chapter 4

WORKLOAD

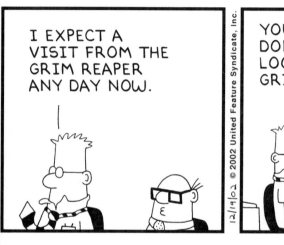

The biggest obstacle to your productivity is your stubborn insistence on being happy. Once you release that, you can get a lot done.

The quality of
your assignments
depends on
your distance from
your boss's office.
Farther is better.

THE KEY TO TEAMWORK is to be a capitalist while convincing your coworkers to be communists.

Knowledge is the same thing as begging for more work with no extra pay. In the event that you develop any knowledge, try to keep it to yourself.

STRATEGIC INCOMPETENCE is like a super power for

deflecting unnecessary work.

AGREE TO EVERYTHING. Do nothing. Blame a vendor.

To avoid work, it's a good idea to create the impression that you are already overloaded. If anyone asks you to do more, just sigh, agree, and say, "I'll throw it on the pile." Wait a week and someone else will cave in and do it for you.

K eep a written list of the excuses you have already used. You don't want to explain why you are having your appendix removed for the second time.

IT'S ONLY POSSIBLE to be creative for a few hours a day. After that, all of your productivity is a form of fatigue-induced dementia that will have to be unscrewed the next day.

Chapter 5

PERFORMANCE AND COMPENSATION

I HAVE NO BUDGET FOR RAISES, SO ALL I CAN OFFER IS AN ATTABOY.

12/27/02 © 2002 United Feature Syndicate, Inc.

THE PROBLEM IS: I DON'T WANT TO CHEAPEN THE WHOLE ATTABOY SYSTEM.

There's always someone willing to do your job for less money. Your only hope is to find a boss who hasn't heard about India.

I NEED YOU TO WORK UNDER THE SEWAGE AND BREATHE THROUGH A STRAW.
I GET A STRAW?!!

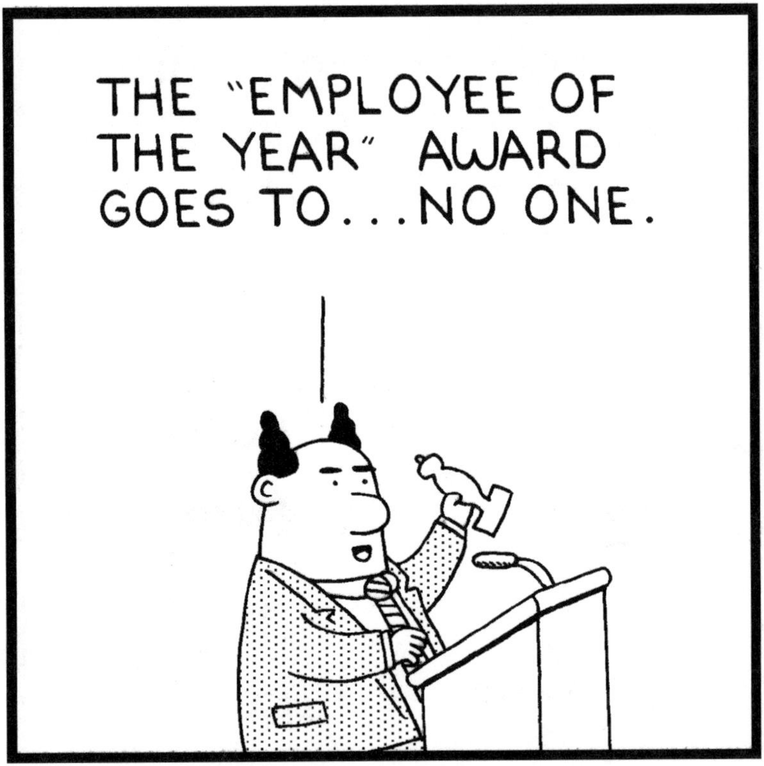
THE "EMPLOYEE OF THE YEAR" AWARD GOES TO...NO ONE.

YOUR BOSS WILL TRY to induce in you a feeling of

worthlessness that is just enough to prevent you from

asking for a raise but not enough for you to quit.

If you can't say
ridiculous things with
a straight face,
there's no room in
management
for you.

The purpose of a performance review is to limit your pay so that your CEO can afford a trophy spouse who enjoys sailing.

The workplace balance of power has shifted somewhat since your parent's day. It used to be that an employer could demand long hours and pay peanuts. Now the employer can demand long hours and pay half a peanut to someone in another country.

YOUR CEO DESERVES to be paid more than you

because very few people are qualified to wait around

until something lucky happens and then take credit.

IF YOU BECOME A CEO, success will be richly rewarded.

So will failure. You won't do too bad in a coma, either.

Management is the art of trading something imaginary for something real.

No matter how many non-monetary incentives you earn, you can never trade them for a new couch.

Chapter 6

B U S I N E S S   E T H I C S

THEN WE'LL BOOK OUR EXPENSES AS CAPITAL, LIE TO THE MEDIA ABOUT OUR PROSPECTS, BRIBE AN INDUSTRY ANALYST, AND CASH OUT!

I KNOW I'M DOING SOMETHING RIGHT WHEN MY BUSINESS PRACTICES GAG A RAT.

AAK AAK AAK

The key to happiness is working with people who deserve your abuse. Otherwise you'll just feel bad while you're doing it.

THE MAIN DIFFERENCE between marketing and fraud is

that criminals have to pay for their own alcohol.

I f you conduct your business in an ethical manner, no one will take advantage of you. That's because you won't have anything to steal.

LYING IS UNETHICAL. Leading people to the wrong

conclusion is competitive.

Honesty is always the best policy for people who have already given their notice and will never need a job reference.

LEADERSHIP IS A FLAVOR of evil. Obviously no

one would need to lead you to do something you

wanted to do anyway.

E mpathy is a sign of weakness. Your coworkers will use it to guilt you into doing their work. When someone routes a Get Well card around the office, your best strategy is to write "Ha Ha!" and sign your name.

t's a good idea to have a credible implied threat to

accompany any request you have of your coworkers.

It helps them focus.

You don't have to hate people to be successful, but it helps.

Chapter 7

BUSINESS COMMUNICATION

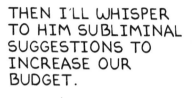

THEN I'LL WHISPER TO HIM SUBLIMINAL SUGGESTIONS TO INCREASE OUR BUDGET.

MORE BUDGET.

KILL THE POINTY-HAIRED MONSTER

IF YOU START MAKING SENSE, people will think you

have no business experience.

Remember that throughout history, the only people who have been wrong are the ones who expressed opinions. Avoid that trap.

THE LESS YOU KNOW, the more you should talk

to make up the difference.

WE'LL INCLUDE A PET GERBIL IN EVERY BOX. WE JUST NEED TO MAKE SURE IT'S IN A SEALED PLASTIC BAG SO IT WON'T CHEW ON THE CABLES.

f you make the mistake of providing useful

information to people, you might as well

paint a target on your forehead.

Instructions should be given verbally and vaguely. Otherwise you lose all powers of deniability.

AVOID ARGUING WITH NUTS. You can't cure them but they can certainly turn you into a nut.

The best way to mock the nonsense that comes out of your boss's mouth is by embracing it enthusiastically. You'll amuse yourself while still looking like a team player.

THERE IS NO IDEA so bad that it cannot be made to look

brilliant with the proper application of fonts and color.

It's a good idea
to discourage people
from talking to you.
Nothing good can
come from that.

Chapter 8

STRATEGY
AND PLANNING

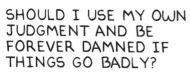

THE PURPOSE OF A PLAN is to disguise the fact that

you have no idea what you should be doing.

A guess is just a guess until you turn it into a pie chart. Then it's an analysis.

You can control your perceived future either by changing what you are doing or changing your assumptions. One of those two approaches is hard.

THE GREAT THING about the future is that you

can't be wrong about it in the present.

IT'S EASY TO IDENTIFY BAD IDEAS. They come from

other people.

E mployees enjoy it when managers pretend to value their input. It's called "getting buy-in" and, although employees will still feel like pimples on the corporation's buttocks, they will be less inclined to complain about the new plan. No one likes a whiney pimple.

No matter how bad are your company's products,

there is some theoretical level of discomfort that

can make your salespeople sell it.

ONLY LOSERS MAKE DECISIONS. Winners wait

for someone else to make a decision so they can point

out its flaws.

STRATEGY IS whatever you are already doing plus a

clever catchphrase that says you will keep doing it.

Chapter 9

MOVING UP

IT'S BETTER for your career to screw up something big

than to succeed in something that no one notices.

SKILLED EMPLOYEES are hard to replace. That's why crooks and imbeciles are promoted to management.

Hard work is rewarding. Taking credit for other people's hard work is rewarding and faster.

The job isn't done until you've blamed someone for the parts that went wrong.

ONCE YOU BECOME A BOSS you are freed from the constraint of knowing what you are talking about.

Management is the art of pretending that idiots can become geniuses if you offer them enough incentive.

The benefits
of having
an assistant will be
outweighed
by that person's
defects.

As a manager you have an obligation to train people in the chain of succession. Make sure those people are bigger morons than you are. Otherwise that succession will happen sooner than you planned.

A MANAGER'S JOB is to allocate resources. A leader's

job is to steal resources. Leaders have bigger houses.

Chapter 10

MOVING ON

Employees are your most valuable asset,

especially when you downsize them to

make your stock options skyrocket.

Consultants try to avoid mentioning the root cause of the company's problems, because that is invariably the people who hired them.

t is considered sporting to give your downsized

employees a severance package to augment the

office supplies they have already stolen.

YOU CAN TRICK EMPLOYEES into quitting without a

severance package by asking them to do things differently.

Change sounds good but it hurts like crazy.

In business, a failure that isn't obvious for a few years is as good as a success.

IF YOU'RE A MORON, try job-hopping. That way you'll have a good excuse for appearing perpetually under-qualified.

The best way to get rid of a deadbeat is to give him a glowing review and then recommend him for a job in another department.

f you have worked at your company longer than the other people in your department, chances are that you are not one of the "good people."

ALWAYS REMEMBER that as long as other people are

gullible, there's no limit to what you can achieve.